Experiencing Miracles, Signs, and Wonders!

Personal Stories of God's Amazing Grace

Ruth Basi Afia-Maetala

PUBLISHED BY

Our Written Lives, LLC

SAN ANTONIO, TEXAS

Second Edition, Limited Printing
Copyright ©2021 ©2023
Ruth Basi Afia-Maetala

ISBN: 978-1-942923-58-9 (paperback)

Editorial Team
Rachael Hartman
Rhonda Reynolds
Destiny Simms

For information, email RMaetala@gmail.com

Or write to Ruth at:
P.O. Box 361
Honiara, Solomon Islands

Unless otherwise noted, Scriptures are from the King James Version, public domain. Any alternate versions used are noted, and belong to the copyright holders thereof.

Cover art and fonts licensed for free use.

Dedication

To my children:

Travis, Loate, Mary-Ellen, Te-Aroha, & Maefasia

Congratulations on your great work and endeavor.
-Shirley Henson, Former Editor of Reflections Magazine

Contents

Acknowledgments	6
A Word From My Husband	8
Foreword	10

1. Miracles _____ 13
2. When Faith is the Substance _____ 17
3. When Jehovah Provides _____ 29
4. Miracles When in Need _____ 35
5. Miracles Through Warfare _____ 41
6. Miracles in the Face of Denial _____ 47
7. Miracles Through Angels _____ 51
8. Faith Airlines _____ 57
9. Grace Miracles _____ 61
10. Jehovah Rapha, My Healer _____ 65

About the Author _____ 72

Acknowledgments

So many times I feel like God is so far away that He cannot reach us. I look up in the dark sky and see the moon and the stars, then I am reminded that God is so close. He allows me to see His creation every day.

The most important acknowledgment I can make goes to Jesus of Nazareth, the Miracle Worker, the very source of my faith. He is surely the One who authors each phenomenon in my life.

History tells me that He calmed the troubled Sea of Galilee and the angry waves obeyed His voice. He gave sight to the blind, raised the dead, the lame walked, He fed the hungry, comforted those who mourn, and taught many of life's lessons. His love was manifested through the things He did and the words He spoke.

When He felt hungry, when He prayed a prayer, and when He died, He tasted of what should have been my judgment—for He saw me beyond the Cross. His charisma,

His leadership, and His life explain why He was God yet He was fully human.

Two thousand years have gone by, and He is still the same. He is awesome and He is faithful. Many now experience His power throughout the world.

I also want to acknowledge some special people in my life, my husband Hennessey Maetala and my children, for their continued understanding and support of the work I am doing.

To my loving grandmother, Ruth Aven Sanga, thank you for being an example in word and deed.

To my friend and mentor, Sister Jean Gordon, thanks for being a prayerful person who is fearless to face life's storms. Your faith and prayer life help me to soar where only eagles fly.

A Word From My Husband

Our God is a miracle-working God. He was the same in Noah's time, in Abraham's time, in Jacob's time and in the present day. Miracles are not constrained by time and cultural boundaries but happen when there is faith present. The environment for a miracle is importantly full of faith.

For example, when Peter and John approached the Gate Beautiful at the hour of prayer, the lame man looked at them with earnest eyes. He had great a need—the ability to walk. He asked for alms instead.

Peter and John were sensitive to his real need—the healing of his legs and the ability to walk normally. It is amazing what happened that day. Peter said, "Silver and gold have I none; but such as I have give I thee: in the name of Jesus Christ of Nazareth rise up and walk" (Acts 3:6). And as Peter took the lame man by the hand, and lifted him up, his feet and ankle bones received strength and immediately he walked. What an occasion for celebration!

Experiencing Miracles . . .

We live in a time in which miracles are rare. This book is proof that Jesus is still in the business of performing miracles in our lives. This is a wellspring of valuable evidence of God's abundant grace and mercy demonstrated through His wonder-working power. We must not confuse ourselves about miracles but we must believe that signs and wonders must follow those who believe.

It is my prayer that you will be blessed by the testimonies shared in this invaluable resource. God bless.

Rev. Hennessey Maetala
Rev. Hennessey Maetala, Pastor
New Hope United Pentecostal Church
Solomon Islands

Foreword

Experiencing Miracles, Signs, and Wonders! Personal Stories of God's Amazing Grace will lift your faith in the God whom we serve.

Jeremiah speaks of the foolish, those without understanding, who have eyes, and see not. Jesus himself spoke of those who have eyes to see but fail to see. Many do not recognize the many miracles of provision, of protection, of health, and of blessing—simply because they are not looking! Their spiritual eyes have failed to focus on what God has done in the past, is doing in the now, and in what He will do in the future!

Habakkuk, the prophet, records in Chapter 2, Verse 2, "Write the vision, and make it plain upon tables, that he may run that readeth it." Ruth Maetala is making available to us an opportunity to see, not what she has done, but what God has done.

May you be blessed with each page. As you read the recorded words, may it give you faith to believe! Faith to run! And faith to know that God does the same for each of us. If we would but open our eyes to see, believe, and accept.

"O LORD, how manifold are thy works! In wisdom hast thou made them all: the Earth is full of thy riches" (Psalm 104:24).

Roger D. Buckland

Roger D. Buckland
UPCI Regional Director / Pacific

Chapter 1

Miracles

Sometimes people question God, saying to themselves, "Will I ever get a miracle?" In these instances, we don't have the faith to receive a miracle, and can actually prevent ourselves from receiving God's mercy and love.

But there are times when God, in His Sovereignty, does a miracle anyway.

In those moments, we have a choice to make. We can run back to Him and fall at His feet, worshiping just like the one leper who came back. Or, we can be like the other nine lepers who never returned to show their gratitude. Many people dismiss miracles as luck or coincidence. They receive the miracle and then walk away without acknowledging the Miracle Worker.

Jesus performed many miracles during His ministry here on earth. He healed the sick, He opened blind eyes, He helped mute people speak, and deaf people hear. He fed the hungry, calmed storms, and raised the dead to life.

These are just some of miracles He performed. You might be wondering, "What exactly is a miracle?"

A miracle is defined by the Oxford dictionary as a wonder or a great phenomenon, which makes anyone who witnesses it marvel at the sensation it causes.

It is often unexpected, happens supernaturally, and works against the laws of nature.

The first miracle Jesus ever performed was at a wedding in Cana. They had a need: they ran out of wine. Jesus met the need: He turned water into the best wine they'd ever tasted. No doubt, this miracle created a sensation among Jesus' followers. After this initial miracle, Jesus continued to do His Father's business by working many more miracles, ultimately bringing glory to His Father through salvation-giving, life-changing phenomenons. Truly, His followers were forever changed as they witnessed Jesus perform miracle after miracle.

Jairus received a miracle for his daughter who was dying. The woman with the issue of blood felt virtue flow into her body as she desperately touched the hem of His garment. Peter's mother-in-law was healed from a fever and Lazarus was raised from the dead. A man with a withered hand had

Miracles

his hand restored. Many afflicted were made whole. Those who were bound were delivered and their sins were forgiven.

Jesus still does miracles today. He calms the sea in people's lives, and heals those who are afflicted by sickness or disease. Demons are cast out. The broken are made whole. You might wonder, "How can this be?" It is Jesus, the Miracle Worker, still working. He is the God who has always existed, even before time began. He is worthy of the glory and the praise. His Name is above every name.

What is the purpose of a miracle? Miracles increase our faith. Miracles lift up the Name of Jesus. Our testimonies give glory to the God who works miracles. It gives others hope that they too can receive something miraculous from God. When we put our faith in the all-powerful, miracle-working God, we will see miracles!

How do we know when a miracle has occurred? It's when a person diagnosed with a condition such as blindness or cancer is made well. Or when an impossible situation turns around with no explanation other than God's divine intervention. The person who has received the miracle now becomes an ex-cancer patient, an ex-criminal, an ex-(fill-in-the-blank). They have a testimony that can point others to the God that helped them.

As you wait on your miracle, remember victory doesn't come easy. It requires faith. Unwavering faith. In the book of Hebrews, Chapter 11, the writer declares, "Faith is the substance of things hope for, the evidence of things not seen." When we have faith, we see beyond our present conditions into a new reality where our need has been met and is now a testimony of God's goodness and ability to help. Then, we know that Jesus is Lord over all things.

I invite you to experience life beyond what you can see with your eyes, or even what your human mind can understand. Jesus said that faith the size of a mustard seed could move mountains.

Will you exercise that faith today?

Chapter 2

When Faith is the Substance

When I travel, I want to feel secure. I want to know where I'm going, how I am going to get there, what hotel I will stay at, how much money I need, and who to contact in the event of an emergency. Sometimes, an ordinary trip can turn into an unexpected and unwanted adventure. Delays and disappointments can leave me feeling defeated or frustrated because things didn't go as planned. Nevertheless, life can change without notice and I must adjust to a new situation.

One such experience I had resulted in me sleeping at an airport in Bangkok, a land foreign to me. I was informed that my hotel fees would be covered, but not my airport transfers. I didn't have money for transport.

Even though sleeping at the airport was inconvenient and uncomfortable, I did glean something from the experience. I noted the dedication of the Muslims praying all around me. They prayed consistently. They were focused and unhindered by what was going on around them. If only Christians prayed in this manner, there's no telling what God would do. As a side note, international airports often feature prayer rooms to meet the needs of travelers. Muslims ran the prayer rooms at this particular airport in Bangkok.

Another memorable travel experience I had was in 2001. It was the first time I traveled to America. I had $50 USD to last throughout my thirty-two-hour trip and my entire stay in the state of Massachusetts. I nearly slept through all of the boarding calls, even when I was sleeping at my terminal in the Los Angeles airport. Thankfully, I made my flight!

There were other shorter trips that provided many challenges. I've slept in several airports. I've hitchhiked in foreign countries. I've had many issues with travel.

When I flew to Fiji for the first time, I went without any money to cover my stay. This trip taught me to put my trust securely in Christ, silencing my internal fears. A couple of days into the trip, a sponsor graciously gave me the funds to cover my stay. While I was there, I learned my way around the city and became familiar with popular landmarks, which further put me at ease.

When Faith is the Substance

Every person's Christian journey looks different, but we all want to be assured that there is some kind of plan, even should the unexpected happen. The plan of salvation presented in Acts 2:38 has clear steps: repent, be baptized in the name of Jesus Christ, and receive the gift of the Holy Ghost. These are the simple steps laid out so that we can begin our Christian journey. When you follow the Bible, you can be assured and secure in your salvation!

Once we've journeyed for some time, unexpected life crises may cause us to question our faith journey. When I was diagnosed with cervical cancer, I had many questions for God, such as, "How can this happen when I've been serving faithfully?" God brought me through that trial in 2009, but I've had many other trials as well.

I realize now that trials are all a part of our journey with Christ. My faith is not based on what I think or feel, but instead on the salvation plan outlined in Acts 2:38 and throughout scripture.

When families go on vacation, they typically save money for the trip. They want to ensure they have finances for food and a hotel. They want to have time and money to go sightseeing or to enjoy local landmarks, museums, or national parks. These special activities create memories that the family can celebrate for years to come.

Wouldn't it be nice if we could plan for our Christian journey and be assured that we have all we need to make it through? We would want to control the trip and the stopping points, but a faith journey isn't like that. We will see sights and have experiences but we don't make the plan; God does.

There will be times of great celebration when Jesus pours out the Holy Ghost to inspire and refresh us for the journey. There will also be times we didn't anticipate or plan for, but we lean on Christ during these times. Perhaps these times result in memories we'd like to forget, rather than remember. Some might even prefer to escape this life altogether. This is when we need to go back to the One who makes the plan. Jesus is Hope for the hopeless and a Friend to the poor and the needy. We must believe He will bring us safely to our destination in great victory.

During my journeys, I came across a particular type of traveler—a backpacker. These people intentionally travel with small amounts of money because they want the adventure of taking risks and finding solutions to problems

When Faith is the Substance

that may arise. To them, traveling is an adventure that must be conquered.

Likewise, we have to be willing to go on an adventure with Jesus. We may not have all the provisions we think we need, but we can trust Him to work it out as we go. The key is to stay prayerful and in communion with the Lord Jesus Christ. This will ensure we complete our journeys.

There are many books on prayer. These are okay to read, but I personally feel the best way to improve and maintain your prayer life is to pray corporately with brothers and sisters in Christ. Pray at family gatherings, and pray the Word. Busy mothers can pray on the way to pick up their children from school. Praying with children is a great idea as well. Family prayer creates a safe space for everyone to share and support each other.

Lately, in my travels, I've seen a lot of people traveling with children. My hubby and I used to do that in our younger days as we traveled to places like New Zealand, Australia, and the United States, taking our children and the Gospel with us as we went. My husband and I were new in the Lord when we first started traveling. We learned important lessons in those early days, making life easier later on.

For instance, in 1998, we planned to go from Fiji to New Zealand. We had some money saved, but not enough for us to feel secure should something unexpected happen. We were taking advantage of a sponsorship opportunity that would allow us to live and study in New Zealand for three years. At the time, we had three small children under seven years old. My husband was a young pastor and sometimes naïve, but he was not afraid of a challenge! Actually, it was his bold faith that weathered the storms of doubt that often swirled around his wife.

Some of you may identify with our experience. You may be a traveling evangelist or teacher. You might not have the support you need to have your children cared for back home while you travel. We didn't either. You might be homeschooling in travel trailers or living in small apartments. We did that. You might be working for a low salary while trying to support the family on long journeys. We did that too.

Through it all, we learned to trust God a little more each day. We adjusted. We were flexible. Our kids ate together, cooked together, fought and cried together. We learned to forgive one another over and over again.

You might think your journey is too difficult and can't be continued. It could be true, but God is there to fill in the gaps for you. During our travels, our children learned to live within our means, enjoying what we could afford. They learned lessons about kindness and hard work, and about supporting missions.

Every journey is full of lessons we can learn. We chose to see things from this perspective. So, if you think your journey is unbearable, look for the lesson in it. What is it God wants you to learn? Turn to your Bible and make sense of God's wisdom, which is sure to shape your decision.

One of our most miraculous experiences during the early traveling years happened in a strange new land, a city called Palmerston North, New Zealand. Shortly after we were settled, God miraculously linked us up with a oneness fellowship group through a Fijian brother named Don.

My husband, in his usual adventure-seeking way, discovered a weekly car auction in Turitea. He came home and announced that he'd just won a car at the auction for $1,700! It sounded too good to be true. We'd have transportation to get back and forth between the school, the hospital, and the market. We wouldn't have to leave our children at home while we traveled. We would have room for everyone.

Reality set in as I realized we were $700 short. We had some tense conversations and wondered what would happen. God used this situation to prove Himself to us in that strange land.

Malachi 3:10 challenges us to prove God with our tithes and offerings. Proving God is not an easy task. As a wife and mother of three kids, living in a new and strange country, it was not easy for me to trust the situation would be okay. It was especially challenging when I recalled a very difficult experience I'd had just the previous year.

The year before, in 1997, we'd had a traumatic experience that left a bad taste in our mouths. Someone tricked us out of our rental deposit of $500 and we ended up sleeping in a room infested with mosquitoes and frogs for almost a month!

Talk about Egyptian plagues in the 21st Century! Been there and experienced it! The memory of those frogs and mosquitoes was fresh in my mind as my husband announced the news about the car auction. I was nervous. I knew the only way we would be able to buy that car within the 24-hour window was through divine intervention. My faith seemed way smaller than the mustard seed size required.

While my faith wavered, my husband held on to his. He gathered the family together and prayed about the situation. I'd overlooked what Paul said to the Corinthian church about a lack of faith being a sin (Romans 14:23). I did not see how it was possible to purchase a vehicle we could not afford.

My husband told me, "God is going to provide." In my mind, I was thinking, "Yeah, yeah, we are going to look foolish when the car is passed on to the next bidder because we couldn't come up with the money." I fully identified with Sarah's situation as she laughed in the tent when God announced she would in fact have the promised son.

As I expected, the next morning dawned and no funds had come in. Calmly, my husband walked in the door at about 8 a.m. and asked me if I could go and withdraw the money from the ATM. Reluctantly, I obeyed. I sauntered to the ATM and entered the pin, expecting nothing, but to my surprise, our balance was exactly $1700! You can imagine my shock. Despite my unbelief, God had given us another miracle!

Maybe some of you reading are in a faith struggle right now. Let my situation remind you, God is able! Remember when Jesus rebuked His disciples in Luke 8:25? "Where is your faith?" He asked them. Then, Jesus rebuked the waves and the wind, and peace was restored.

Would you believe I still struggled in my faith even after seeing the $1700 balance? I had to find the source of the extra money. I couldn't accept the idea that God had made a deposit into our account. I called the International student's office, then I went to the University campus bank. There was no trace of a $700 deposit. I then printed a bank statement so I could verify it wasn't a fluke or a bank error. The statement did not show a deposit at all. Still, dissatisfied, I decided to call my father-in-law in the Solomon Islands. He too denied sending the money.

Finally, I humbled myself and repented before God. I begged for His forgiveness as I finally accepted the truth. It was a divine miracle! We bought the car and it remained in great condition from 1998-2000. I will never forget how God came through for us that day. It changed me forever.

When Faith is the Substance

In his book titled *Writings Vol. I*, Reverend Bill Davis spoke about how hard it is to get rid of things in our lives when we are used to them. He said it is easy to put on the new, but ridding ourselves of the old is usually painful because it causes change and requires adjustments. As I view my situation through the light of Reverend Bill Davis' revelation, I see myself getting rid of old worldly behavior in exchange for a heart that pleases God.

In my previous mindset, I believed the miracles of the Bible were for the disciples and those living in Bible days, but God challenged my beliefs. If He could turn water into wine (John 2:9), or raise Lazarus from the dead (John 11:43-44), He has the power to do a miracle in my life today!

The purpose of miracles is to give God the glory. This is my reason for sharing my experiences. Sometimes, we might feel the Bible is a book full of bedtime stories. Or, maybe we think miracles only happened back then. I used to think like that, but God proved me wrong. He is the same yesterday, today, and forever! Amen!

Chapter 3

When Jehovah Provides

In 1 Kings, 17:7, as the widow of Zarephath used up all of the food she had for her son and herself, her mind had to have been full of questions. I wonder if she felt it was the end of the world. Perhaps she thought it was the end of their lives.

When the prophet asked her to feed him she said, "I have not a cake, but an handful of meal in a barrel, and a little oil in a cruse: and, behold, I am gathering two sticks, that I may go in and dress it for me and my son, that we may eat it and die" (I Kings 17:12).

In the midst of her fear, she stepped out in faith. Everything in her life was riding on the One true God. As she stepped out of the norm and took a big risk, guess what happened? God didn't let the oil or the flour run out. There was more in the buckets every time it was needed. It was a miracle!

Experiencing Miracles . . .

I'm here to tell you, miracles still happen even to this day! Often our faith is as short-sighted as the widow's. We cannot see very far beyond our need. Jesus wants us to practice our faith and see what He is capable of doing in our lives. Never put limits on Jesus!

Jesus' first wedding was also where he performed his first miracle. The celebration was about to face an interruption; the wine was running out. Mary, Jesus' mother, knew who He was and what He could do. She knew in her heart Jesus was the Messiah, and He was on site. She told the servants do whatever Jesus told them to do (John 2:1-12). As a result, Jesus turned ordinary water into the best wine.

In 2003, God put it in my heart to put my faith into action. God showed me the sacrifice of Abraham found in Genesis 22. God provided for Abraham because of his act of obedience. As I read that testimony miracle of provision, God showed me the animal caught in the bush was a proper supply for Abraham's sacrifice.

I wanted to put what I learned into action. I had to make myself available to do God's work, despite any needs I might have. In one of the services at Eastview UPC, Pastor David Hunt requested people to make pledges so the church could buy a new sound system. The one in the church needed to be replaced.

My faith rose! I made a pledge of $200 during that service. Did I have the money? No. I learned how to *give by faith*. Such faith shuts out every negative thought and question. You don't know how what you need is going to happen, but you know it will. Faith is saying and believing what you need will happen—no matter what the circumstances may look like. Faith is stepping out when you'd don't know how what you need will happen.

The Holy Ghost was so strong that Sunday night when I made the pledge. I knew without a shadow of a doubt God was speaking to me. I committed to giving $200, and God was going to provide.

The scripture the Pastor used in the sermon that night was the story of Abraham preparing to offer Isaac as a sacrifice. As I listened to the sermon, I felt a sense of clarity and confirmation.

God then spoke to my heart and said, "Give, and I will provide the sacrifice." Looking back, I believe the experience was a test of my faith. Would I have enough faith to make a sacrificial offering to support the house of God?

Experiencing Miracles . . .

I didn't have any money, none at all. I was once again living in a strange country, and I didn't have anyone who could lend me any money. I didn't even know if there was a lending service around. In fact, I didn't even have a bank account. With all odds against me and my miracle money, I kept my eyes on Jesus. I did not falter in my faith, but I knew I'd know what to do at the right time.

According to the Bible school calendar that week there was a scheduled three-day fast. That Monday, the college fasted as a whole. I joined in on the fast. On the third day of the college fast, something unimaginable happened—a miracle. Praise the Lord!

It was Thursday at about 12:30 in the afternoon. As we were walking passed our car, we saw an envelope laying in the driver's seat. It was addressed, "To the Maetalas."

The car was locked! So how did an envelope get in there? Did someone break in? It didn't matter. That envelope held my miracle money!

Human limitations will say, "It is impossible." Faith says, "With God all things are possible" (Matthew 19:26).

Paul encourages us to walk by faith and not by sight (2 Corinthians 5:7). In our bodies we are limited by what we

When Jehovah Provides

feel, taste, smell, and see. When there's no sign of hope, it is very difficult to believe, but Jesus can perform miracles out of nothing!

During our ministry, we went through many times of not having any money, but we were never hungry. We learned very quickly in that when the King of Kings is onsite, His promise is sure! What He says is final. Although it may be insignificant, if He says it, then it will happen just as He said.

Chapter 4

Miracles When in Need

In Genesis, when Sarah asked Abraham to send the bondwoman away from their home, Abraham took action. According to Abraham, Sarah was his wife. He was committed. He did not want to cause further heartache. He felt caught between his wife and her bondwoman, the mother of his son. He chose Sarah and gave up his son and the servant.

As result, Hagar left with a wounded and broken heart (Genesis 21:16). Her hands must have been heavy as she collected her son Ishmael's things. She might have packed slowly, and fumbled trying to put sandals on Ishmael's rugged feet. The bag she carried may have felt like 200 pounds of unwanted weight.

In today's civilization, I imagine Hagar would have had to leave an abundance of clothes, a washer and dryer, a bedroom graced with lace curtains that hang to the floor. She would have to leave a comfortable couch and footrest, and all of Ishmael's toys and clothes. Trying to carry all of that would be unbearable and impossible.

Suddenly, Hagar had a revelation. The reality was, she was no longer wanted! She could no longer live in the house with Abraham and Sarah. Her days of slavery and bondage were over. She was free to go!

This was not the way she planned her road to freedom! It was not her dream to become a homeless, solo mom. Her freedom did not guarantee food, clothing, or shelter. Her son lost his inheritance. She must have felt empty and confused.

Didn't anyone remember it was Sarah's idea for her to conceive Abraham's son? Did anyone actually care? Sarah's attitude seemed spiteful. The pregnancy was all Sarah's idea and now she was angry about it. The thought of wandering in the wilderness alone with a fatherless son felt a million times unbearable.

Hagar needed a miracle, and at the point of her need, the LORD responded. God's angel said, "Hagar why do you weep? Look yonder and find water for yourself and the lad" (Genesis 21:12-20). What a relief!

Miracles When in Need

At the point of our need, Jesus is always there. Look at God, providing again! If He feeds the sparrows daily, why worry?

Once, my husband was working on our little house. We were both in full-time ministry and the home project was challenging in many ways. That day, he was hammering nails into something when he heard a knock on the door. A stranger was there and told him that he brought the money we needed for the house. He handed over $1,000 Solomon dollars and went on his way.

Another time we had a need beyond our means, a miracle happened again. This was on Thanksgiving Day. We were Bible College students and were without food. As a mother, I was worried because my kids were still at school and I did not want them to come home when I didn't have food to offer.

I turned desperately to God in prayer. About an hour before my family came home, I heard a knock on the door. I went to answer and met a lady at door. She looked down at a list and said, "Is this 104-A Mary Ann Street?"

Answering, I said, "Yes."

She walked back to the white van parked in the driveway and brought out a box of food. She gave it to me, then turned to her paper again and placed a check mark next to our address. She left without saying any more.

Excitedly, I took the box of food into the house. As I unpacked the box, I counted every item with care and gratefulness. It was all we needed for a good Thanksgiving dinner: turkey, milk, water, beans, stuffing, croutons, fruits, butter, and more.

Once again, the Holy Ghost reminded me when He says, "He will never leave and never forsake" then He will NEVER leave or forsake. He will make a way! Let's worship Him for who He is and what He has done!

When God provides He knows what we need. Before going back to the Solomon Islands from the States, we had to pay our bills at Bible School. We were in Missouri for the weekend. Brother Maetala preached on Sunday morning at the Maxwell's church in Gerald, Missouri.

Sister Kay Maxwell told my husband we would all visit Brother Masters' church that evening. My husband accepted the invitation and we tagged along.

Miracles When in Need

When we arrived at Brother Masters' church, he told my husband he was going to preach! We did not expect anything massive, but we were fixing to see something massive! Praise the Lord!

Although he did not expect to preach, my husband willingly accepted. During the service, the Holy Ghost moved mightily.

At the end of the service, my children were down at the altar praying with a man who was seeking the Holy Ghost. While the altar service was going on, Brother Masters' stopped all the praying and said, "Let's collect an offering for this family."

Some people responded and Pastor Masters' said, "Thank you." After some time, he said, "We need to give another offering."

Suddenly, the Spirit of giving was upon the Church, and one by one people came up and gave what was in their hands. That night more than $4,000 was collected. That was just what we needed for our final school bill at Texas Bible College before graduation in May 2006.

What a miracle! We have lived to experience again and again that God keeps His promises! He will not leave or forsake us. He is JEHOVAH JIREH—our provider.

We all have a need at some point. In the face of desperation, God is our Way Maker. Who can stop God from traveling through time and across international boundaries? No one. God provides and He does it in His time. His timing is never too late!

Chapter 5

Miracles Through Warfare

When you do the work of God, you're going to face spiritual warfare. A period of spiritual combat is tiresome and often puts pressure on our faith. Our comfort is in the Word of God that exhorts us to fight with mighty spiritual weapons, not through fleshly strength, but powerful through God. It is God's power that pulls down strongholds. Through faith, we reject vain imaginations and submit our thoughts to the power and authority of the Holy Spirit.

"The weapons we fight with are not physical weapons. On the contrary, they have divine power to demolish strongholds. We demolish arguments and every pretension that sets itself up against the knowledge of God, and we take captive every thought to make it obedient to Christ. And we will be ready to punish every act of disobedience, once your obedience is complete" (II Corinthians 10:4-6 NIV.)

During a spiritual battle, we will often see signs, or manifestations, of spiritual activity that alert us that an evil spirit is at work. I don't discount the forces that are against us. There are plenty of examples in the Bible of demonic activity. Think about the story of the seven sons of Sceva who drove out evil spirits in Acts 19:14. Think about the demon-possessed man, living in the tombs of the Gadarenes, often breaking shackles and being driven into an isolated wilderness (Luke 8:26-39). These scriptures teach us we must fight the spiritual enemy with spiritual weapons of warfare. One such weapon is prayer.

I have a story of the delivering power of prayer. A lady approached Pastor Maetala one day during a teacher's training in 2009. As she walked up to him, she suffered a spiritual attack. Her body twisted and she experienced what we would call "a fit." She began to foam at the mouth. My husband commanded this spirit in the name of Jesus to go and return from where it came.

The evil spirit immediately left. A few days later, the sister came and spoke with us. She told us someone had come to her house and apologized to her. "They sent magic to kill me," she said. "That man told me he was almost killed by that same magic on the same day you prayed for me and I was delivered!"

...Through Warfare

That was not the only such case we experienced. In October 2010, we went through ten days of spiritual warfare. God delivered our daughter, Loate, from spiritual attacks. At midnight for ten nights in a row, a demon walked into our house, tormenting Loate. The demon induced her to fear, telling her she was going to die. She would cry and scream. We fought that deceiver every night. On the tenth night, the devil left as we prayed, "In the name of Jesus, go back to the pits of hell where you came from!" After that event, we lead the church into a season of deep prayer and fasting. We understood the power of spiritual warfare in the name of Jesus!

I think it's natural that people want to experience miracles, but sometimes miracles require work. A miracle may require spending hours in prayer and days in fasting. What is the most important thing of all to remember? Jesus intercedes for us when we are spiritually weak. The battle is not ours, but His!

In Romans 8:26-27 NIV, Paul's encouragement was, "In the same way, the Spirit helps us in our weakness. We do not know what we ought to pray for, but the Spirit himself intercedes for us through wordless groans. And he who searches our hearts knows the mind of the Spirit, because the Spirit intercedes for God's people in accordance with the will of God."

Jesus warned his apostles about this in the Gospels. Some things only come out through prayer and fasting. We cannot receive the miracles we need if our minds and imaginations are not surrendered to the authority of the Holy Ghost.

Then there was that story in the book of Mathew. A man approached Jesus and said, "Your disciples prayed for my son, but the devil could not leave." Jesus answered, "This kind will only go out by prayer and fasting."

We often want a miracle. We want deliverance, but we do not want to fast and position ourselves to take our rightful place in God. We don't want to humble ourselves by depriving ourselves of food. What are you willing to do to receive your miracle?

We need to humble ourselves, asking God for His cleansing power as King David did. He said, "Wash me thoroughly from mine iniquity, and cleanse me from my sin. For I acknowledge my transgressions: and my sin is ever before me" (Psalm 51:2-3 KJV). Our God is glorified in bad

...Through Warfare

situations where He shows himself strong. Even though at times we've had to deal with stubborn or deceitful spirits, Jesus is always our Victor!

It was not a mistake that Jesus approached Genesareth. There he saw a man filled with demons, living amongst the dead. He cut his body as the demons called out to Jesus not to send them away. At that moment, Jesus knew the man needed a miracle. He needed freedom and deliverance. Jesus responded by commanding the demons to go into the pigs. As a result, the suicidal spirit that left the man drove the pigs into the ocean.

When we are bound by the problems and habits of life, we must be willing to let Jesus come to do the work we need Him to do in our lives. In Revelation 3:20, we have an invitation to open the door of our hearts to Him who is willing to come in and eat with us. In most cultures, eating together promotes peace. It builds relationships. It allows a free flow of conversation. It is a personal time of engagement and interaction.

If we ignore His invitation, we will suffer consequences. Like the man Jesus met in the tombs, we might wander all our lives, living in the same spot, the same environment, and blind to the opportunity we have to start a relationship with God. The chains that bind us may leave us wandering among our dead past.

If you are reading this line and feel you are bound, if you feel hopeless because you are wandering about your in past, if you think that there is no hope and freedom for you . . . I can tell you now there is One who is knocking at the door of your heart.

He is Jesus of Nazareth and He is waiting on you to respond to that knock. He desires to be in your house and eat with you and have a personal relationship with you.

Don't stay stuck in the graveyards living with unnamed headstones and empty tombs. Pick yourself up and answer the question. It might just be your day to find freedom in Jesus.

Chapter 6

Miracles in the Face of Denial

People pushed on both sides to get closer to Jesus. They were there to glean from his teachings. All of a sudden, He turned as He heard His disciples and followers telling her off.

"Don't disturb the Rabbi. He is teaching. Don't come near! You are an outcast! He doesn't have time for you!"

The Greek woman was persistent. She cried aloud to the King of Kings, "I need help! My daughter is sorely vexed with a devil."

Jesus denied her request. He told her that what He has is for the House of Israel and not for outcasts. He said His power was for His children. Countering His rejection, the woman bravely answered, "Yes, but the dogs eat the crumbs that fall from under the master's table."

Oh, what bravery. Oh, what determination. Due to her consistency and worship, Master Jesus awarded her complete healing for her daughter.

What a lesson for us! We must learn to put our faith into action and worship our way through denial. We must believe and trust Jesus will win the battle for us, even when it seems all hope is lost and the answer is, "No."

I remember not so long ago, one of our local pastors was attacked by a demonic spirit in the early morning hours. Around 4 a.m., the Holy Ghost woke me up to pray for the man and his wife. I interceded. All I knew was that the man was wrestling in the spirit, and his wife was out traveling in the province somewhere.

As dawn broke, the pastor's wife called my husband. My husband rushed to their house and found the man lying on the floor, throwing up blood. As he prayed for the pastor, my husband took him to the hospital and left him in the care of the medical system.

Praise God for His all-powerful Name, because the pastor was saved, and his health restored in just a couple of days! Miracles only happen when we have a need. That pastor had a need and he received a miracle!

Prayer and perseverance are vital for a miracle to come. We can't give up when things look bad, and when it seems our requests have been denied. We must step out in faith

...in the Face of Denial

and exercise our trust in a God whose hand is not short concerning His promises.

When we need something from God, we must keep the faith to receive it. We must not waver. Our faith must be accompanied by action. We should not turn away from God when the conditions aren't suitable to our liking.

The Greek woman worshiped Jesus in the open, right in front of the crowd, down in the dirty, dusty road. No matter how they looked at her, she was determined. She was humiliated in public by the words Jesus spoke. She did not care, nor did she give up.

Miracles require more than just ordinary prayer. There must be a deep persistent moan that demonstrates our desperation for an answer. It takes humility no matter where you are, in public or in private. When our faith is tested to the breaking point, then we know our miracle is a prayer away.

Chapter 7

Miracles Through Angels

The angel Gabriel announced the miracle birth of Jesus Christ. Gabriel had to obey orders from the Captain of the Host of the Heavenly armies. The mission was important. Jesus would save the world from the sin it inherited from the Garden of Eden.

Mary, the mother of Jesus, the Savior of our world, was amazed at the fact God chose her to be bear His son. "How can this be?" she asked Gabriel when she heard the unexpected tidings.

Naturally, we desire miracles, but how often do we think about angels being involved in our miracles? Angels are often associated with miracles.

At times we lose faith and miss out on opportunities for God's miracle power to manifest in our lives. During such times, we let our minds run. We hope for miracles, but it's easy to become spiritually stagnant. When a miracle happens, we dismiss it and write it off as a coincidence.

As Apostolic believers, we must guard our hearts from such states. We must have faith that God has sent His angels around us, and miracles are happening around us daily.

Sometimes when a miracle happens, it feels like a roadblock. You may be driving and something delayed your journey, like an unexpected flat or a missed flight. It might feel like things aren't going your way, but it just might be a miracle to save you from an unexpected accident or death.

I have a friend at church, Sister Margaret, who walked home one early Saturday morning. The Holy Ghost told her one word, "cross." She listened and crossed the road. A few seconds later, a cab wrecked at the very spot she had been standing.

Just like Peter in prison, tied by chains between two soldiers, your situation may seem beyond impossible. Have faith and hope in Jesus. An angel might be sent your way, to show you a way out!

I know it's hard to accept delays. It is difficult to consider the fact that a delay could be the conduit through which a miracle would flow. Maybe there is an angel pushing you out of harm's way. It might be an angel like Gabriel or a person who knocked at your door. God can use anyone to accomplish His will. Whomever God sends will have the answer for your situation.

In Christmas of 2005, we were faced with moving overseas again. We had just moved three years ago and we had to move again. I had questions about whether my children would have a normal life, or if they would live like gypsies on the mission field. This time we were moving to New Zealand to do some short-term mission work. So who knows, I thought, maybe our plans might be short-circuited again.

As a mother, I was anxious, worried, and fearful because I wanted to know how things would work out. I needed security! I wanted to be assured we would not go hungry, that our needs would be met, that my husband would be the man God designed him to be and that our contributions to the mission field would be worth the sacrifice.

I foresaw the risks in terms of our future, although I knew without a doubt God would provide. Although my husband encouraged me, I still wanted to know what would happen, and what we would do. Financially, I could not see a way our move could happen in less than three months.

I asked God, "Please show me a sign." I waited.

Christmas Eve that year, 2005, came quickly. We were picking up the children from something they were doing at the church and I felt in the Holy Ghost it would be our last night (at least for a long time) to go and see the Christmas lights in Lufkin, Texas. Instead of driving to Lufkin, we chose to head to Nacogdoches to see the lights this time.

"I have some money to buy sandwiches at Jack in the Box on Highway 59, and we can eat while on the road," I said to my husband. He agreed and we headed off to see the lights.

Christmas lights, here we come! The lights in Nacogdoches were breathtaking! The Bethlehem scene stole the center of my attention. I stood there reflecting on Jesus' birth. I could feel God's presence as we got out of the vehicle and walked toward the lights. Our three older children were with me so I started telling them the Christmas story.

My husband and Tearoha were slowly picking up the pace a little further away from us. As we stood there in awe of the lights, a white van drove up. The driver stopped next to my children and asked if I was their mother.

Excitedly, my kids chorused, "Yes!" A lady hopped down from the driver's seat and came around, opening the door of the van, and reaching inside. She tugged out two bags and put them on the sidewalk.

Then she turned to the kids and said, "Merry Christmas!" Immediately she hopped back in her van and drove away.

The kids went hysterical. They called out, "Ma, look! "Mom, this is for us."

Their continuous happy shouts drew my attention in their direction. I knew right away these gifts were my sign from God. He would provide.

In short, when we ask God for a sign, will He turn His back on us? A million times no! He will give us what we need when we ask in His Name. Jesus visited us to let us know He will make a way to the islands where we were going.

I know some of you may have had a similar experience. Just when we thought we needed a miracle, we got one: a human angel. The fact is, humans can enable miracles in our lives just like God's heavenly messengers.

Hold fast to the Word when it says, "Do not forget to show hospitality to strangers, for by so doing some people have shown hospitality to angels without knowing it" (Hebrews 13:12).

Chapter 8

Faith Airlines

I'm so fascinated by the fact that each winter swans fly south to the warm weather of the Southern Hemisphere. When I see these birds fly, I see miracles in flight.

I'm also fascinated by eagles. I read about them as they soar and their wings rest upon God's astonishing ability to keep them in the air. They are miracles in the air.

The robin hops a short distance but still does not fall from a tree. It's a miracle of its own!

The sky is the limit for birds. Some can do summersaults or spin. Some have the ability to sing, and others to screech. It amazes me that they can still have enough air to sing as they are flying through the sky.

Flying is fun. As an international traveler, I'm always aware of distances and flight times. I know flights are costly, particularly in some remote areas of the world. Flying the red-eye and saving up airline miles helps, but air travel is very expensive. More recently, flights to the islands have

Experiencing Miracles...

become increasingly cheaper, but not cheap enough for the middle working class, much less for pastors or missionaries. Flying isn't easy when you don't have a lot of money.

I often think . . . it's truly a wonder that I can sit on an airplane for hours in the sky! When the plane touches down I have this amazing feeling that "I survived!"

One year, my family was going to Fiji. My ticket was paid by a scholarship; however, the scholarship did not cover my husband's or children's tickets.

My husband was headed to Fiji for the Suva Bible School. I was on my last day of work at the New Zealand High Commission office. It was the day before we flew, but my husband still didn't have a ticket to travel. As the clock ticked that day, I become more and more anxious. I felt butterflies in my stomach. I felt nauseated throughout the day about it.

As I was closing up that day, my boss at work approached me to say goodbye. She handed me an envelope. In that envelope, there was a round-trip ticket from the Solomon Islands to Fiji and back; it had my husband's name on it! I went home and looked at my husband, "Pack your bags!" I said as I handed him his ticket.

Faith Airlines

God was gracious. We boarded the flight and off we went. It was a miracle flight, one we could have never done without the help of Jesus Christ.

Sister Sarah Prince, my long-time sister in the Lord and a close friend, recently shared her testimony about how she received an airline ticket by faith. She was to attend a lady's conference and was invited to be the main speaker for the conference in the Solomon Islands.

She was to travel from Auckland, New Zealand, but she didn't have a ticket. She testified that she walked confidently into the travel agent's office and asked directly for the air ticket. The travel agent handed her a red packet of travel documents and said, "Go to the Solomon Islands and come back with good news!"

Oh, Praise Jesus!

In January of this year, our church sent four students to Fiji for Bible College. One of the students was not able to pay for his airfare. The students would be leaving with Brother Maetala in three days, but the one had no ticket.

At the leaders' meeting, one of the church members gave a Miscellaneous Counter Order (MCO) from Solomon

Airlines. It was his family's unused annual travel money, a total of SI $9,000. It was enough to pay for two tickets.

Look! What a mighty God we serve!

Chapter 9

Grace Miracles

When my family attended Eastview Church in Lufkin, Texas, we had an opportunity to meet a young, mentally challenged woman named Angela. Her favorite color was red and she would always dress in bright red. Every time we saw her, that's what she was wearing. She loved special treatment and attention.

It didn't take us long to get to know Angela. We called her "Angie." We always made it a point to take her home after church services when she was able to attend. We especially tried to take care of her when she was trying to get the attention of important people at the church. Sometimes her love of attention would annoy people, and we wanted to do what we could to help bring peace to the situation.

On one of the trips we took Angela home, she wanted a quick stop by the Seven-Eleven. She went inside the store by herself. We waited for some time in the car, until my husband asked me if I could go in and check on her.

To my utmost dismay, when I walked inside I saw Angie fully engaged scratching a lotto ticket as if no one was waiting on her. With a lot of effort, we finally got her back in our van and to her house.

We often ask ourselves why God put people like Angie on our path. It was difficult. God did get our attention, although we were not fully attentive to what He was saying at the time. As I'm thinking and writing about miracles, God brought Angie to mind.

Sometimes, Angie's communication was not all that great. I remember once she became angry with my kids. I also remember them laughing together at other times. Sometimes Angie's perfume was very strong. Oftentimes, I felt as if she wanted something more than just going to church. She wanted love, to be treated normally, and to belong.

There were many times Angela would become angry about something. She had no concept of personal space. At times she even insisted on preaching the sermon herself! Despite all of her ways, we saw miracles when we allowed her into our lives. And we gained a friend.

Grace Miracles

Too often we, as Apostolics, undermine our faith when we look to experience great miracles. We have physical sight but cannot recognize the miracle of the sight we take for granted. We have life, but don't recognize our daily life is a miracle!

Naturally, some of us seek for miraculous, great, and powerful things God can do. Instead of miracles, we find ourselves guilty of attitudinal issues when we act like Pharisees and Sadducees. We allow ourselves to be absorbed in our own small worlds, our daily routines, and the rut of life happenings. We don't realize that miracles are all around us, every day! If only we would choose to see the daily miracles!

If our faith is low and we experience no miracles at all, Hebrews 11:6 reminds us that "without faith, it is impossible to see God." With faith, we can see God everywhere, and miracles in all of the daily blessings around us.

It's important to know the Miracle Worker. When God performs miracles, it is for a purpose. When we have respect for the Miracle Worker, and faith and trust in Him, we can stand and enjoy the grandeur of the God of miracles.

Experiencing Miracles...

Angie's life has helped me to focus on all of the little miracles in my life. Through Angie, and practicing grace with her, God helped me to appreciate a simple friendship that has brought many miracles into my life.

Sometimes the pain and frustration we feel when we go out of our way may seem like a curse rather than a blessing, but when you really think of a miracle as a supernatural phenomenon, you will not question when miracles occur in your life. To grow and ripen in Jesus is a miracle. Being delivered and set free from your old ways is a miracle.

At times, we felt somewhat frustrated in trying to understand Angie's speech impediment during the first months of her acquaintance. We faced mistreatment a few times as we chauffeured home when we faced drunken relatives who were not impressed with what our church was about. None of these challenges compare to God's miracle-working power in our lives. His grace working through us is its own miracle!

All the little things in life matter. From the air inside of our lungs to the food on our table, from the roof above our heads to the shoes on our feet, and the strength we have each day to get out of bed. Don't forget to enjoy God's creations. Open your eyes, it's all around us. Let all things be a reminder of who He is!

Chapter 10

Jehovah Rapha, My Healer

I often wonder what it felt like when the virtue of Jesus left him during the healing process of the woman with a blood problem (Luke 8). I also try to imagine how the woman felt when she received her healing, just by touching the hem of Jesus' garment. The unnamed woman was so desperate for the Healer to heal her. There was something about the faith she had in Jesus, which drew her closer to Him.

I imagine her as she pushed between the high and mighty, the lofty people who saw her struggling to draw near the Healer of all diseases. I can picture some of the women in the crowd acting snobbish toward her, wishing she would leave before Jesus saw her, before she made a scene.

I see her struggling to keep her tears from falling down her dirty unwashed face. I imagine she was holding the bottom of her dress pushing through the crowd, trying not to fall down, trying to make it to Jesus. Just imagine the odor of her clothes from bleeding for so many years—unsanitary! Still, she pushed on through the crowd despite rejection from the disciples. There was no obstacle that could keep her away. Amen!

I see her having big faith—unmovable faith—which is how she even made it to Jesus. Her fingers trembled to reach the hem of Jesus' garment. Then it happened! She touched Jesus. Oh, what hope!

In 2009, I received a medical report that showed all the signs of cervical cancer. I repeated a few tests to prove the science behind it. When I heard the news, I was very discouraged. I cried throughout the entire night. My sadness turned into pain and resentment.

Oftentimes, I'd become negative about how I saw my situation. I could only see death. Unlike the unnamed woman, I lacked faith. My life became difficult. I wanted to just be alone, by myself. Despite my attitude, I continued to praise God and encourage myself, even when I knew both my faith and my body were weak.

One day while traveling on business to one of the outer islands. God convicted me and led me in an Esther

Jehovah Rapha, My Healer

fast (three days without food or water). I came out of that fast renewed. I read Psalm 118:17, in which David said confidently, "I shall not die, but live, and declare the works of the LORD."

That was the confidence I wanted to possess. I wanted a strong enough belief to nurture and grow my faith. Faith can overpower all diseases and conditions. I don't want to take life for granted. I want to encourage you to believe and to have faith beyond all sickness, all diseases, and all conditions. I want you to know 100%, God is more than able. He is the all-sufficient One!

I prayed a great deal and God did what was unthinkable. He always shows up and shows out. I had to have a biopsy done before surgery in January 2011. In December, my doctor called me and said my situation was not life-threatening. I felt my faith come to life.

"I am healed in Jesus' Name! Oh, great is thy faithfulness!" My faith sprang into life and I could see the light. I could understand what God wanted to do in my life. He gave me a testimony. He gave me a miracle!

Sometimes God uses us to show us who He is and what He can do. It's all for the kingdom of God. He gets all the glory. It is a miracle—a phenomenon! Although I cannot physically see what the Great Doctor Jesus has said, I have faith and I know I'm healed in His Name.

If David can say with confidence that God knows all the members of the body (Psalm 139:13-14), it means He knows every part! Whether it's an eye, a foot, or a fingernail, Jesus knows every one of us in detail. Praise be, and glory to God in the highest!

I want to encourage everyone. You will never know the resurrection power of Jesus until you experience His mercy in your life. You may not experience my type of healing with an absence of faith. We cannot experience the authority of Jesus' Name if we are not baptized in Jesus' Name (Acts 2:38). I want to experience all God has to offer. I want to have a bold heart, like the Lion of Judah. When and if all hell breaks lose, I want to be able to praise Him through all the storms of life—just like I learned to praise Him through my healing process.

While I was writing this book, Rusi, a Fijian brother in Christ, offered to pay for gas for my husband to do some lawn care at the church one Saturday. Accompanied

Jehovah Rapha, My Healer

by two other brothers from our church, Rusi and my husband went to the gas station, gas can in hand.

A stranger sitting in his truck at the gas station told the man to fill up the can with fuel and he would pay for it. The two brothers from our church witnessed the goodness of God at that very moment. They returned to the church full of excitement. They talked about this blessing for several days.

Where you are and what you are going through doesn't matter when it comes to Jesus. Where you lack, He will make a way. Everything happens in His perfect timing. He is the same yesterday, today, and forever.

Be encouraged! Be of good cheer! If and when you need a miracle, God has the ability to meet all of your needs. Jesus is the only Miracle Worker and there is power in His Name.

By His stripes, we are healed! (Isaiah 53:5)

Be still and know He is God! (Psalm 64:10)

Many scriptures point to healing and promises. One that greatly encourages me is Psalm 118:17 NIV, which says, "I will not die but live, and will proclaim what the LORD has done."

This is a promise to me and all of you who are facing any difficult situation. Do not be disheartened or distraught. We need to proclaim all the mighty acts He has done for us. Our testimonies can save someone and can build or restore someone's faith—or our own. It gives hope when there is no hope. That is our purpose—to live and declare His works.

Praise the Lord!

About the Author

Ruth Basi Afia-Maetala

Ruth Maetala is a native of the Solomon Islands. She was born and raised in a family of six children. The only daughter in the family, Ruth learned life is a journey of both faith and struggle. Ruth is a pastor's wife, a mother, and a grandmother.

She graduated with a degree in Women's Studies and Social Anthropology from Massey University in New Zealand. She has a diploma in Christian Education from Texas Bible College in Lufkin, Texas, USA.

She is a development specialist by profession and has served in several administrative roles. In the Kingdom of God, she has served in various mission capacities in several countries.

She is currently serving as the ladies' ministry leader for the United Pentecostal Church of the Solomon Islands. She is passionate about mentoring young women leaders, young wives, and mothers.

Ruth is an author and international speaker. Her works have been published by SAGE, Australian National University, Auckland University of Technology, and other publications.

For information, email:
RMaetala@gmail.com

Or write to Ruth at:
P.O. Box 361
Honiara, Solomon Islands

www.OurWrittenLives.com